ATTRIBUTES OF GOD

MADE EASY

Attributes of God Made Easy

Published by Rose Publishing
An imprint of Tyndale House Ministries
Carol Stream, Illinois
rose-publishing.com

The Made Easy series is a collection of concise, pocket-sized books that summarize key biblical teachings and provide clear, user-friendly explanations to common questions about the Christian faith. Find more Made Easy books at rose-publishing.com.

ISBN 979-8-4005-0377-1

Author: Mike Nappa, MA in Bible and Theology, Calvin Theological Seminary; BA in Christian Education, Biola University; author of the award-winning commentary *Bible-Smart Matthew*. To learn more, visit MikeNappa.com.

Printed in the United States of America
July 2025, 1st printing

CONTENTS

INTRODUCTION

The first time Samuel met the professor, he received a dead fish, preserved in yellow alcohol, with instructions to "Look at it." That was it.

It was the mid-1860s, and Samuel Scudder was a new student of Louis Agassiz, one of the foremost zoology professors at Harvard University. His first assignment for Samuel was simply to stare at the dead fish for a while. Samuel was at a loss, but still he spent a good ten minutes studying the *Haemulon* until he'd seen everything there was to see. When he had finished, though, his teacher was gone! Frustrated, he returned to looking at the fish—turning it over, counting its scales, even pushing his fingers down its throat. Anything to pass the time until the professor returned.

Finally, late in the day, Professor Agassiz came back. Young Samuel proudly recited all the fishy discoveries he had made during the boring, drawn-out day. But the professor frowned and said, "You have not looked very carefully. Look again, look again!" And that became his lesson plan for the next three days. For hours and hours on end, Samuel's only assignment from the great zoologist was "Look, look, look!"

At the end of that week Samuel realized he'd unexpectedly become an expert on *Haemulon* fish—in an extremely short amount of time! He'd gained more knowledge than he thought was even imaginable, just by taking extended time to "Look, look, look!" at his subject. And he finally understood the incredible power of intense observation that Professor Agassiz had been trying to teach him. "That was the best entomological lesson I ever had," Scudder later wrote, "a lesson whose influence was extended to the details of every subsequent study."[1]

Studying God is just a little bit like Scudder's study of the fish: When we invest the time to "Look, look, look!" we can unearth new discoveries *every single time* we gaze in God's direction.

Through our sustained glimpses at the attributes of God as revealed in the Bible, we learn about him: his nature, his character, his actions, his priorities, and his preferences. In doing so, we unveil something of who he is and what he does. Our task, though, is not to amass a supposed complete knowledge of God through a study of his attributes—but simply to look at him with an unwavering gaze. In those moments, we continue to discover anew the splendor of the limitless one whom we worship.

HOW TO USE THIS BOOK

You may want to read the entries in this book consecutively from start to finish. You may prefer to skip around, studying the entries by topic or as they relate to your particular circumstances. The entries are arranged alphabetically—feel free to thumb through as works best for you. This book is designed to be *useful* to you, not to make you conform to it.

The attributes included are not an exhaustive list; they are representative of the most well-known aspects of God and a fascinating place to begin—and from which to continue—a lifelong study of God. Also, the question we're pursuing in this book is not "What is God like?" but something more akin to what theologian A. W. Tozer asked: "What has God disclosed about Himself that the reverent reason can comprehend?"[2] Our source for answers to that question will be the Bible.

Here's what you'll find in each entry:

Attribute Name

These are best read in the context of one of two phrases: "God who is" or "God who possesses." When you read the attribute love, you can understand it as "God who is love." However, when reading the attribute compassion, you can say, "God who possesses compassion." This distinction will become more natural as you read through the book.

When discussing an attribute, it is important to remember God's Trinitarian nature—the idea that although distinct from each other, God the Father, the Son, and the Holy Spirit are one. Therefore, attributes applied to one person of the Trinity will apply to all three persons of the Trinity.

Category

When studying God's attributes, it can help to think of them in categories, as Bible scholars do. Most attributes fit into several categories, and some categories overlap.

Absolute—These attributes of God are not present in any way in anything he has created.

Emanant—These attributes of God flow through him and are seen in his acts of creation.

Moral—These attributes of God have to do with his righteous interactions with people.

Natural—These attributes of God have to do with the ways he governs the physical universe.

Relative—These attributes of God are present, to a degree, in humans, who are made in his image.

Is—These attributes describe God's character—who he *is*.

Does—These attributes describe God's activity in the world and in our lives—what he *does*.

Description

Here's where you'll find a few key Scriptures, as well as insight into what the attribute means when applied to God.

Bottom Line

This is a short, final thought that summarizes the attribute.

For Further Study

This lists some Scriptures you can look up to discover more about what the Bible says regarding this attribute.

Related to

This is a short list of some other attributes of God related to the one being described.

All right—you're ready! Turn the page and begin looking at God through the lens of his remarkable attributes.

AUTONOMY

RELATIVE

IS

"Our God is in the heavens, and he does as he wishes."

PSALM 115:3

"He does as he pleases among the angels of heaven and among the people of the earth. No one can stop him or say to him, 'What do you mean by doing these things?'"

DANIEL 4:35

When we say that God possesses autonomy, what we mean is basically this: *God does whatever he wants to do*. This also means that he cannot be coerced into doing anything he doesn't want to do. He answers to no one. In all the universe, God alone is completely independent in his decision making and activity.

The autonomy of God is intertwined with his authority, his unchallengeable right to exercise his will over anything that he created—which is, indeed, *everything*. Paul described this aspect of God using the image of a potter: "When a potter makes jars out of clay, doesn't he have a right to use the same lump of clay to make one jar for decoration and another to throw garbage into?" (Romans 9:21). The Greek word translated as "right" is *exousian*, and it speaks, not only to the ability to make a decision, but also to the power to enforce whatever decision is made.[3]

There are two interesting implications of God's autonomy. First, we learn from both history and Scripture that God is constantly delegating lesser degrees of his absolute authority to humans—from kings and presidents to parents and even to individuals. This leaves open the possibility that his extended authority can be misused by us. That, as you no doubt have seen, can be tragic. Our only hope, then, must lie in complete trust in the promise of Romans 8:28: "We know that God causes everything to work together for the good of those who love God and are called according to his purpose for them."

Second, although no one can tell God what to do, he has chosen to obligate himself to our well-being anyway. As Peter wrote, "He has given us great and precious promises" (2 Peter 1:4). Through his many promises in Scripture, God has made himself *accountable to himself* in order to realize our eternal best interests, regardless of our temporary circumstance. That is both undeserved—and unbelievably kind.

Bottom Line: God doesn't need your permission to do whatever he wants to do in your life and circumstances. He will accomplish what's best for you—whether you agree with him or not.

For further study: Deuteronomy 32:39; Job 42:1–2; Psalm 135:6; Proverbs 19:21; Jeremiah 32:27; Romans 9:19–21; Ephesians 1:11

Related to: Omnipotent, Sovereign

BEAUTY

EMANANT

RELATIVE

IS

DOES

"One thing I ask from the Lord, this only do I seek: that I may dwell in the house of the Lord all the days of my life, to gaze on the beauty of the Lord and to seek him in his temple."

Psalm 27:4 NIV

"God has made everything beautiful for its own time."

Ecclesiastes 3:11

What is beauty, exactly? And why would we say that God—who by definition cannot be seen with human eyes—is beautiful?

Common opinion today is that beauty is entirely subjective or in the eye of the beholder. Yet Scripture indicates that God possesses an objective beauty—regardless of the beholder—that is unmatched by anything we can see or know in this life. David sang of that in Psalm 27 (above), using the Hebrew root word for beauty, *noam*, usually understood as meaning something pleasant or delightful.

Beauty appears to serve no practical purpose in the natural world, offering no protection, nourishment, or any other advantage. The only explanation for it—and the uniquely human ability to delight in it—is that it reflects a beautiful Creator who is active in our world.[4]

The beauty of God is one of his attributes that describe both something that *he is* and something that *he does*. We cannot look at his personal beauty; we're simply incapable of seeing into that spiritual realm, and it could be that his beauty is so overwhelming that it would be lethal to us (Exodus 33:20). However, beauty is also an emanant attribute of God; it's something that flows from him, through him, and with which he saturates creation. This is why we can weep at the sight of a stunning sunset or marvel at shining stars scattered across our night sky or delight in the laughter of a child. It is also why we, as individual beholders, can find something beautiful that others might consider ugly.

So what is beauty, exactly? It's everything we know as pleasant and delightful, combined with more than we can even imagine to be beautiful. And beauty is only possible because it exists eternally in God himself.

Bottom Line: The beauty in your world is proof of the beauty God possesses—and shares.

For further study: Job 26:13; Psalms 90:17 (KJV); 135:3; Ecclesiastes 3:11; Isaiah 28:5; 33:17

Related to: Glory, Perfect

COMPASSION

MORAL RELATIVE DOES

"The LORD passed in front of Moses, calling out, 'Yahweh! The LORD! The God of compassion and mercy! I am slow to anger and filled with unfailing love and faithfulness.'"

EXODUS 34:6

"Jesus saw the huge crowd as he stepped from the boat, and he had compassion on them because they were like sheep without a shepherd."

MARK 6:34

It's impossible to overstate the fact that when God described himself to Moses, the first word in his description was *compassion*. Compassion, at its heart, is the active desire to alleviate another's pain; yet, when God called himself compassionate, *he* was the one who had been harmed. Exodus 32–34 gives us the situation.

God had recently freed the Israelite people from slavery in Egypt. Huddled together in the desert, they had been waiting for Moses to speak privately to God, and they got impatient. (They didn't know that God was, at that time, giving Moses the Ten Commandments.) The Israelites created a false god (a golden calf) and began to worship that inanimate thing by offering sacrifices, getting drunk, and engaging "in pagan revelry" (Exodus 32:6). This "pagan revelry"—which is a polite way of saying it—was a terrible, terrible sin. Such irreverence cost the lives of at least 3,000 people and caused a great plague.

And then ...

In the aftermath of that horror and betrayal by the people of Israel, God spoke to Moses and said of himself, "The Lord! The God of compassion and mercy!" (Exodus 34:6).

That was more than just a description of deity; it was, and still is, an inviolable promise of God toward humanity. The Israelites had broken trust with God—right after he had set them free. And yes, there were consequences but not the destruction they deserved, because God himself chose compassion instead of retribution. The choice to show compassion over retribution was proved once and for all with the sacrifice of Christ on the cross for us.

So when we say that God possesses compassion, it's not just a pretty way of saying "He's so nice, isn't he?" Rather, God's compassion is a deliberate act on his part. In his compassion, he chose to send Jesus to be sacrificed for us—and it cost him dearly. Which we would do well to remember.

Bottom Line: Our multitude of sins have made us undeserving of God's great compassion; yet he gives it nonetheless. Why? Because from the creation to today, *compassion* is what God chooses to be known for.

For further study: Exodus 33:4; 2 Chronicles 36:15; Psalms 51:1; 86:15; 103:8, 13; 145:9; Lamentations 3:32; Joel 2:13; Matthew 14:14; Luke 6:36; James 5:11

Related to: Grace, Love, Mercy, Patient, Redeemer

CREATOR

"In the beginning God created the heavens and the earth."

GENESIS 1:1

"Through [Christ] God created everything in the heavenly realms and on earth. He made the things we can see and the things we can't see—such as thrones, kingdoms, rulers, and authorities in the unseen world. Everything was created through him and for him. He existed before anything else, and he holds all creation together."

COLOSSIANS 1:16–17

God *made us*, and everything we can and cannot see, as well.

It's not popular today to admit that we have a Creator who both initiated and sustains the universe in which we live. But Scripture reveals this truth: "The LORD is God! He made us, and we are his" (Psalm 100:3).

No one knows all the details, and scientists rightly study to better understand the mechanisms of creation, but here's what we do know: Once there was nothing. Then there was something—an entire cosmos from which has sprung uncountable measures of life and being, both physical and spiritual, massive and microscopic, seen and unseen.

Genesis 1:1 tells us this was the conscious act of a divine Creator. The Hebrew word used is *elohim bara* with the first word meaning "God" and the second being a technical term meaning "create." In the entire Old Testament, every time the word *bara* (create) occurs, God is always the subject. For all the writers of the Hebrew Scriptures, it was apparently a settled idea that creation *ex nihilo* (out of nothing) was an act that only God could do.

For that alone, God deserves our worship, our service, our lives.

Bottom Line: "You are worthy, O Lord our God, to receive glory and honor and power. For you created all things, and they exist because you created what you pleased" (Revelation 4:11).

For further study: Genesis 1–2; Nehemiah 9:6; Job 38–39; Isaiah 42:5; Jeremiah 51:15; John 1:1–4; Ephesians 2:10; Hebrews 11:3

Related to: Father, Omnipotent

ETERNAL

"Have you never heard? Have you never understood? The Lord is the everlasting God, the Creator of all the earth."

Isaiah 40:28

"You must not forget this one thing, dear friends: A day is like a thousand years to the Lord, and a thousand years is like a day."

2 Peter 3:8

When we say that God is eternal, we don't mean to imply simply that he lives for all time. Rather, we mean that *time itself is irrelevant to God*, that he existed before time was created, and that he will continue to exist when time no longer does. He alone is without beginning and without end. Or, as Revelation 4:8 states, God is the only one "who was, and is, and is to come" (NIV).

This can be hard for us to grasp, since we are bound so strictly by the constraints of time.

We are born, we live, we die. No so with God. He lives but is never born and never dies, except in his incarnation as Jesus. Although he observes the passing of time with us, he exists outside of time and therefore isn't swept up into the succession of minutes that pile one upon the other. He doesn't sit today wondering what tomorrow will hold, nor does he look into tomorrow and lose sight of every detail of the past. *Future* and *past* are words that only have relevance to humans; the eternal God sees and understands all of time as "everlasting now"[5] and is able to intervene and act with eternal intent at any moment in time.

Bottom Line: Time exists only because God created it. God, alone, exists unbound by time.

For further study: Deuteronomy 33:27; 1 Chronicles 16:36; Psalms 90:2; 93:2; 102:25–27; 1 Timothy 1:17; Jude 25; Revelation 1:8

Related to: Immutable, Self-Existent

FAITHFUL

"Understand, therefore, that the LORD your God is indeed God. He is the faithful God who keeps his covenant for a thousand generations."

DEUTERONOMY 7:9

"God is faithful. He will not allow the temptation to be more than you can stand. When you are tempted, he will show you a way out so that you can endure."

1 CORINTHIANS 10:13

How can we be confident that God will keep the promises he made in Scripture? Because he is faithful. How can we know that God will not stop loving us? Because he is faithful. How can we be sure that God won't forget us, won't abandon us, won't misplace us, will always do what's best for us, will always fill and empower us, will always reward us according to his word?

Because he is *faithful.*

God promised to deliver his people, the Israelites, from slavery in Egypt—and he did (Exodus 6:6–8). He promised to make David king over Israel—and he did (1 Samuel 16:1–13; 2 Samuel 5:1–4). He promised to send a Messiah to save people from their sins—and he did: Jesus fulfilled that great promise (Isaiah 7:14; Matthew 1:20–25; Luke 2).

It is the faithfulness of God that ensures our destiny with him, that keeps safe our trust in him. In the biblical context, God's faithfulness carries two primary meanings. First, he is completely reliable, trustworthy, and loyal. He won't forget his promises (Deuteronomy 4:31; Hebrews 10:23); he won't sleep through our need (Psalm 121:3–4); he won't leave us to face the troubles of this life alone (Hebrews 13:5–6). Second, the faithfulness of God means that his love for us is unfailing—everlasting in eternity and constant in each moment (Psalm 143:8; Romans 8:35–39). This is shown supremely in his promise to save sinners (Matthew 1:21), Jesus's redeeming death and resurrection (Hebrews 13:20), and his Holy Spirit's continual work of sanctification within us (Hebrews 13:21; Philippians 1:6).

One caution, though. Because God is faithful, he will only do what is in your best interests—not necessarily what you think is best. His faithfulness works in conjunction with his attributes of being good, just, patient, and wise. Thus, he will patiently work goodness and justice in your life, according to his infinite wisdom, not your limited understanding. That means he will surely allow you to experience pain and disappointment so that he can faithfully use them to bring about what's absolutely best for you, both here and in eternity to come.

Bottom Line: God can always be trusted—even when you don't like what he does.

For further study: Exodus 34:6; Deuteronomy 32:4; Psalms 115:1; 146:6; Isaiah 49:7; Lamentations 3:22–23; 1 Corinthians 1:9; 2 Thessalonians 3:3; Hebrews 10:23

Related to: Good, Just, Patient, Wise

FATHER

MORAL RELATIVE IS

"Are we not all children of the same Father? Are we not all created by the same God?"

Malachi 2:10

"See how very much our Father loves us, for he calls us his children, and that is what we are!"

1 John 3:1

One of the most powerful images of God in Scripture is found in the parable of the prodigal son (Luke 15:11–32). In this story, the almighty, eternal God is described as a loving, patient, generous *father* who celebrates when his wayward son to returns home. Pastor Ray Ortlund explains the significance of that perspective this way: "That God the Father has made himself God our Father means that he is personally, emotionally, and even sacrificially involved with us."[6]

The Hebrew word used for father is *ab* and the Greek word is *pater*. Both mean roughly the same thing: "one who originates life and nurtures it as a parent."

The Bible describes different ways of understanding God as Father:

- God is the Father or life-giver to *all* of humanity (Numbers 16:22; Ephesians 3:14–15).
- God is also the Father of the nation and peoples of Israel (Exodus 4:22; Hosea 1:10).
- God is the adoptive father of all who place their faith in him (John 1:12–13; Romans 8:15–17).
- And, in a way that's both mysterious and separate from the others, God is the Father of the Son (Matthew 3:17; Luke 1:35).

It's important to understand that God could have called himself simply "Almighty" or "King" or "Master of Everything"—because he is indeed all those things. Yet when he wanted to tell us who we are to him, he chose to call himself Father and make us his children. That kind of intimate, familial relationship between Creator and the created is both astonishing and precious.

Bottom Line: God has made himself your father. Therefore, you can genuinely call him, "Abba, Father" (Galatians 4:6).

For further study: Psalms 68:5; 103:13; Isaiah 63:16; 64:8; Malachi 1:6; Matthew 6:9; Luke 9:34–36; John 14:8–11; 16:28; Romans 8:15–17; Ephesians 4:5–6; Philippians 4:20; Hebrews 12:9

Related to: Creator, Love, Patient

GLORY

EMANANT

RELATIVE

DOES

"Who is like you among the gods, O Lord—glorious in holiness, awesome in splendor, performing great wonders?"

Exodus 15:11

"The city has no need of sun or moon, for the glory of God illuminates the city, and the Lamb is its light."

Revelation 21:23

The "glory of the Lord" is an abstract concept that the Bible describes with various expressions. Although we have difficulty grasping the concept, there are some things that we can say about it:

- God's glory is associated with holiness, uniqueness, and the working of wonders (Exodus 15:11).
- It was described by the Israelites who saw it firsthand as "a consuming fire" (Exodus 24:17).
- The glory of the Lord had a physical presence and power that usually prevented anyone from approaching it (Exodus 40:34–35; 1 Kings 8:11).
- It fills the planet (Numbers 14:21; Isaiah 6:3) and the heavens above, what we call outer space (Psalm 19:1).

- And importantly, the glory of God is described as a physical, amazingly bright light that signals his presence (Isaiah 60:1–2; Matthew 17:1–2; Revelation 21:23).

The glory of the Lord is mentioned frequently in the story of the exodus from Egypt. The main Hebrew words used in that story, often translated with "glory," are *adar*, meaning "great" (Exodus 15:11), *kabowd*, meaning "honor" or "splendor" (Exodus 24:17), and similarly, *kabad* meaning "heavy" or "weighty" (Exodus 14:4). In the New Testament, *doxa*, used more than 100 times, is the word we translate as "glory," and it means literally, "what evokes *good opinion*, i.e. that something has *inherent, intrinsic worth*."[7]

In summary, the glory of the Lord is a magnificent and natural expression of his overwhelming beauty and moral rightness, which is eternally awe inspiring and deserving of praise.

Bottom Line: God's glory is an inescapable element of the nature of God—and a blinding reminder that he alone is worthy of your worship.

For further study: Deuteronomy 5:24; Psalms 8:1; 29:2–3; 111:3; Isaiah 6:1–4; Habakkuk 2:14; John 17:22; 2 Peter 1:17; Revelation 5:13

Related to: Beauty, Righteous

GOOD

"The Lord is good, a strong refuge when trouble comes. He is close to those who trust in him."

NAHUM 1:7

"Whatever is good and perfect is a gift coming down to us from God our Father, who created all the lights in the heavens."

JAMES 1:17

One of the reasons that God can be trusted is because he is good.

This aspect of God guides everything he does—his every interaction with us and more. If he was not good, we could have no hope and our faith would be reduced to something akin to ancient pagan worship that sought to appease its gods. It is God's goodness that allows us to befriend him and know him as our Father.

So God is good, and this is true, but what does that mean?

In the simplest, most practical terms, the goodness of God means we can trust that he always acts and thinks with our best interests in mind (Romans 8:28, 31). However, we mustn't assume this can be translated as

"God is always ***nice***." He will always do what's in our best interest—even if we must experience pain in the short term so that we can experience joy in the long term. In this way, his goodness can be compared to the physician who insists on the pain of surgery in order to heal the trauma of serious sickness or injury.

Still, the goodness of God is more than just that simple definition. A. W. Tozer spoke of the all-encompassing aspect of this attribute, saying:

> The goodness of God is that which disposes Him to be kind, cordial, benevolent, and full of good will toward men. He is tenderhearted and of quick sympathy, and His unfailing attitude toward all moral beings is open, frank, and friendly.... The greatness of God rouses fear within us, but His goodness encourages us not to be afraid of Him.[8]

Because God is good, he is also truthful. He can be trusted. He is wise and helpful, patient and forgiving, just yet also merciful. He is our friend and Father—not our enemy and dictator. He is, in every aspect of his being, always and in every circumstance, *good*.

This, then, is our good God—and why he can always, *always* be trusted.

Bottom Line: God is good. All the time.

For further study: 2 Chronicles 5:13; Psalms 34:8; 73:1; 106:1; 145:9; Lamentations 3:25; Matthew 7:11; Acts 14:16–17; 2 Peter 1:3

Related to: Faithful, Joyful, Just

GRACE

MORAL RELATIVE DOES

"The Lord God is our sun and our shield. He gives us grace and glory. The Lord will withhold no good thing from those who do what is right."

Psalm 84:11

"God saved you by his grace when you believed. And you can't take credit for this; it is a gift from God. Salvation is not a reward for the good things we have done, so none of us can boast about it."

Ephesians 2:8–9

To begin to understand grace as an attribute of God, let's look at two examples from Scripture.

In 2 Kings 5, we read the history of Naaman, a general in the army of Israel's longtime enemy, the kingdom of Aram. Naaman suffered from leprosy and, prompted by a Hebrew slave taken in war, he went to Israel to ask the prophet Elisha for healing. Naaman worshiped pagan gods, had killed and enslaved Israelites, and insulted God's people and places. Then God healed him. Completely. At no cost whatsoever.

When we look at the New Testament, Acts 9:1–31 reports that Saul (later called Paul) was the enemy of the followers of Jesus. Saul had imprisoned many and was on a crusade to arrest any he might find in the city of Damascus. Then God stopped him in his tracks, spoke to him personally, called him out of his sin, and redeemed his life. God used this former enemy as the first great Christian theologian.

In both these situations we see the same thing: God's kindness lavished on people who didn't deserve it one little bit. And that's what it means when we say God possesses grace—that he freely gives to us, not what we deserve (punishment), but what we could never earn (kindness). Theologians call that unmerited favor, but it's really just God being himself, acting generously (physically, spiritually, and eternally) toward those who don't deserve it—friends and enemies alike.

Bottom Line: You can never do anything to earn or deserve God's grace, but you can accept it and live gratefully as a result!

For further study: Nehemiah 9:16–17, 31; Psalm 116:5 (NIV); Zechariah 12:10; Romans 11:5–6; 2 Corinthians 12:9; Titus 2:11–14; Hebrews 4:16

Related to: Compassion, Mercy

HOLY

RELATIVE

IS

"Holy, holy, holy is the LORD of Heaven's Armies! The whole earth is filled with his glory!"

ISAIAH 6:3

"You must be holy in everything you do, just as God who chose you is holy."

1 PETER 1:15

The idea that God is holy is a central message throughout the Bible. Both the Hebrew and Greek words translated as "holy" convey the idea of being set apart—particularly in regard to sin. Lawrence Richards explained that something is holy when "it is removed from the realm of the common and moved to the sphere of the sacred."[9]

In this way, the holiness of God is an emphatic declaration of God's absolute sinless purity—his unspoiled righteousness that sets him apart from any created thing. This means God alone holds the ultimate moral authority because of his impenetrable, eternal holy nature. Similarly, everything associated with God is to be holy—such as the Sabbath day (Exodus 20:8–11), Mount Sinai where God had appeared (Exodus 19:23), and the followers of Jesus (Romans 1:7).

The implications of God's holiness are far-reaching:

- In Scripture, those who are confronted with the holy presence of God, are immediately aware of, and ashamed of, personal sin (Isaiah 6:1–6; Luke 5:8).
- Because God is sinless and set apart, all of his other attributes are also sinless—his justice, his love, his jealousy, his goodness, and so on. Every single aspect of God's dealings with humanity is always morally perfect because he is completely holy and sinless in his being.
- We're called to live holy, sinless lives simply because he is holy. Due to our sin we regularly fail. But we can still be made holy because Jesus was sinless and, through his death and resurrection, broke sin's power over us.
- God's own Holy Spirit gives us the daily wisdom and power we need to pursue a holy life. He is more than capable of doing this for us, because he is holy.

Bottom Line: The holiness of God means that he is completely untouched by sin and that he will help you pursue a holy life as well.

For further study: Exodus 15:11; Leviticus 19:2; 20:26; 1 Samuel 2:2; Job 34:12; Psalm 99:5, 9; Mark 1:24; 1 Peter 1:14–16; 2:22; Revelation 4:8

Related to: Perfect, Righteous, Truth

IMMANENT

"O Lord, you have examined my heart and know everything about me.... You go before me and follow me. You place your hand of blessing on my head."

Psalm 139:1, 5

"Jesus replied, 'My Father is always working, and so am I.'"

John 5:17

When we say that God is *immanent*, we mean that he is always alert and active in his creation and in our lives. (Note that this term, *immanent*, shouldn't be confused with the similar sounding *imminent*, which generally refers to something about to happen and is often used when talking about Jesus's second coming.)

Because God is constantly involved in the natural workings of our existence, some have mistakenly taken his immanence to mean either *pantheism* or *deism*. Pantheism equates creation with God, which means that he doesn't exist outside of his creation. This is reflected in statements such as "The universe wants me to do this!" Deism credits God with creating the world but then assumes that he is no longer active in it; his creation continues to move forward like a well-built machine. Both of these views are grave misunderstandings of the immanence of God.

The truth is exactly what Jesus proclaimed: Our heavenly Father is always working in our lives and in his universe. Although he is outside the created order, he still chooses to work within it. His activity can be seen on a universal scale as he maintains our solar system, on a planetary scale through seasons and world systems, on a human scale in the blood that courses through our bodies, down to the microscopic scale of white blood cells that fight infection. Better yet, God's Holy Spirit is constantly at work in the spiritual transformation of his people, helping each of us to discover more of him and how to live well for him.

This topic could be explored in depth in many, many books! But for our purposes, God's immanence is best summarized this way: "God's presence and activity within nature, human nature, and history."[10]

Bottom Line: God is constantly at work in the world and in your life.

For further study: Deuteronomy 4:7; Job 34:14–15; Psalm 33:18–20; Matthew 6:26–33; Acts 17:28; Romans 11:36; 1 Corinthians 12:4–6; Colossians 1:17

Related to: Omnipotent, Omnipresent

IMMUTABLE

ABSOLUTE IS

"I am the Lord, and I do not change."

Malachi 3:6

"Jesus Christ is the same yesterday, today, and forever."

Hebrews 13:8

Immutable is just an academic word theologians use to express the truth that God does not change—ever.

Closely tied to his eternality, the immutability of God is constant because God exists outside of time. His nature and being are unaffected by the past, present, or future, so who he is in that "eternal now" is who he always is (was, and will be) within our past, present, and future. Because of this unchangeable nature, God will never break a promise, never become powerless to fulfill his will, never stop loving, and so on.

But the Bible does teach that although God himself does not change, he does sometimes change his intended actions in response to prayer or other human actions, like repentance (Genesis 6:5–7; Exodus 32:9–14; Jonah 3:10). But this doesn't mean that God is changeable. We should be careful not to confuse who God is with his actions in a particular situation. Also keep in mind that while we may see only two options in a situation, God in his infinite wisdom sees innumerable ways of bringing about his purpose. So, for instance, when God chose not to destroy Nineveh in response to the people's repentance (Jonah 3), that didn't change who he is or his purpose for those who prayed for mercy. It simply changed one possible course of action to another, both of which were consistent with his immutable character and fulfilled his unchanging purpose.

In short, immutability teaches us that God is God, and he always will be.

Bottom Line: God is the same faithful one today that you trusted yesterday, and he will still be faithful tomorrow—fully worthy of your faith in him for all time.

For further study: Psalms 33:11; 102:25–27; Proverbs 19:21; Isaiah 46:9–11; Matthew 24:35; Hebrews 6:17–18; James 1:17

Related to: Eternal, Infinite

INFINITE

ABSOLUTE

IS

"Great is the LORD! He is most worthy of praise! No one can measure his greatness."

PSALM 145:3

"Oh, how great are God's riches and wisdom and knowledge! How impossible it is for us to understand his decisions and his ways."

ROMANS 11:33

The infinite aspect of God is, by definition, more than we can understand using finite language and reasoning. What we can understand from Scripture is that *God is limitless* in his being and ability, *and he is unable to be measured* by any human standard, including time and space. This also encompasses God's *transcendence*—that he is outside his creation, above and beyond all that we can imagine.

Because God's limitlessness is true, it is also—to the utmost extent—a defining element of every one of his attributes, even those not explored in this book. Is God autonomous? Then he possesses limitless autonomy. Is God good? Then he is infinitely good. Is God joyful? Then he is boundlessly joyful. Likewise, he's inexhaustibly wise, unfathomably perfect, and on and on. When examining the infinite nature of God, A. W. Tozer once had to stop in awe and admit, "In the awful abyss of the divine Being may lie attributes of which we know nothing and which can have no meaning for us."[11]

For those of us who are finite, the practical result is that God is never going to run out of anything he has promised; he is always able to lavish his love on us in many, many ways and for all time.

Bottom Line: Whatever you think of God is not enough; he is *always more* than you can reason or imagine.

For further study: 1 Kings 8:27; Nehemiah 9:5; Psalm 147:4–5; Isaiah 40:28; Jeremiah 32:27; Matthew 19:26; Mark 14:36; 1 Corinthians 2:9; Ephesians 3:20; 1 Timothy 6:15–16

Related to: Immutable, Omnipotent, Self-Existent, Spirit, Ungendered

INVISIBLE

ABSOLUTE IS

"The Lord spoke to you from the heart of the fire. You heard the sound of his words but didn't see his form; there was only a voice."

Deuteronomy 4:12

"No one has ever seen God. But if we love each other, God lives in us, and his love is brought to full expression in us."

1 John 4:12

Ah, finally an easy one. Saying that God is invisible simply means that he can't be seen by human eyes. All done, right?

Well, not exactly.

Scripture is abundantly clear that God is invisible—this is related to the truth that he is Spirit (John 4:24), and humans are unable to see into the spirit realm. But the Bible also indicates that some in history *have* actually seen God. Hagar claimed to have seen God (Genesis 16:13); Moses is reported to have seen him on several occasions (Exodus 3:6; 33:11–34:8; Deuteronomy 34:10); and Isaiah and John both claimed to have seen God in the spirit realm (Isaiah 6:1–5; Revelation 4).

So what is going on here? Was John lying when he said, "No one has ever seen God," (1 John 4:12) or when he said, "I was in the Spirit, and I saw a throne in heaven and [God] sitting on it" (Revelation 4:2)?

The answer is that John wasn't lying either time, since both statements are true.

God is invisible in the sense that he exists without a body, as Spirit. And yet, at times God chose to make himself seen in temporary forms visible to humans. And, as theologian Wayne Grudem teaches, "Although God's total essence will never be able to be seen by us, God still reveals himself to us through visible, created things."[12]

God in his true Spirit essence is unseeable, but at times he chooses to miraculously reveal himself in physical forms that can be understood by humans. This is what was going on when he spoke to Moses from a burning bush or gave prophetic visions to Isaiah and John, and so on.

So yes, God is invisible—except when he chooses not to be.

Bottom Line: God has made it possible for you to see him. When you study Jesus, you can see God.

For further study: Deuteronomy 4:15; Job 9:5–11; John 1:18; 6:46; Colossians 1:15; 1 Timothy 1:17; 6:16

Related to: Spirit, Trinity

JEALOUS

MORAL

RELATIVE

IS

"I, the LORD *your God, am a jealous God who will not tolerate your affection for any other gods."*

EXODUS 20:5

"You adulterous people, don't you know that friendship with the world means enmity against God? Therefore, anyone who chooses to be a friend of the world becomes an enemy of God. Or do you think Scripture says without reason that he jealously longs for the spirit he has caused to dwell in us?"

JAMES 4:4–5 NIV

Both these Bible passages speak to the fact that God is a jealous God. But the New Testament tells us, "Jealousy and selfishness are not God's kind of wisdom. Such things are earthly, unspiritual, and demonic" (James 3:15). How do we reconcile this seeming contradiction? How can a jealous God be holy and good, if jealousy itself is "earthly, unspiritual, and demonic"?

It appears that in the Bible, the word *jealousy* has different applications. To help us see that more clearly, let's do a quick sampling of how jealousy is seen in Scripture.

Human Jealousy	God's Jealousy
Provokes sinful attitudes and actions (Prov. 6:34)	Seeks to prevent sinful attitudes and actions (Ex. 34:14)
Acts unjustly (Acts 5:16–18)	Acts to bring about justice (1 Kings 14:22–26 (NIV); Ezek. 16:35–42)
Seeks revenge against the innocent (Acts 7:9)	Seeks redemption for the guilty (Deut. 4:23–31; Joel 2:12–20)
Is covetous (Prov. 12:12; Jas. 4:2)	Seeks to give blessing (Ex. 20:5–6)

The Hebrew word used for jealous is *qanna*, and the Greek word is usually a variant of *phthonos* or *zeloo*. All three words carry roughly the same meaning: "to be jealous, or envious, or filled with zeal." Human jealousy leans pretty heavily into the idea of envy acted out in sin, while God's jealousy is better described as zeal acted out in justice. Human jealousy seems to be a sinful corruption of God's holy passion for faithful devotion to all that is right and good and life giving.

Bottom Line: God is jealously passionate about your spiritual well-being.

For further study: Ezekiel 8:1–18; 1 Corinthians 10:22; 2 Corinthians 11:2

Related to: Just, Righteous, Wrath

JOYFUL

MORAL RELATIVE IS

"Don't be dejected and sad, for the joy of the Lord is your strength!"

NEHEMIAH 8:10

"I have told you these things so that you will be filled with my joy. Yes, your joy will overflow!"

JOHN 15:11

If you've ever wondered if God is joyful, look no further than the Jewish calendar. You'll find that God created numerous feasts, festivals, and celebrations specifically for his people to enjoy.

These national holidays were times for thanksgiving; for providing relief for the poor; and (of course) for music, dancing, wonderful food, and heartfelt religious observances. These are just some of the joyful festivals that the Israelites were commanded by God to celebrate:

- *Passover/Pesach* This is a time to remember the Israelites' miraculous liberation from slavery in Egypt (Exodus 12:1–51; Leviticus 23:5–8).
- *Pentecost/Shavuot* Held fifty days after Passover, this is a time to celebrate the first harvest and to remember

God's gift of the Law to Moses (Exodus 19; Leviticus 23:15–21). (Christian Pentecost marks the giving of the Holy Spirit in Acts 2:1–47.)

- *Feast of Trumpets/Rosh Hashanah* This is the Jewish celebration the New Year and God's creation of the world (Leviticus 23:23–25; Numbers 29:1–6).
- *Feast of Tabernacles/Sukkot* A celebratory reminder of the forty years the Israelites spent in the wilderness before entering the promised land (Leviticus 23:33–36, 39–44).

There were also new moon festivals; pilgrimage festivals; public celebrations of military victories and the coronation of kings; even sheep-shearing festivals! Perhaps most grand of all was the Year of Jubilee, celebrated only once every fifty years. God established this for releasing slaves, canceling debt, and returning all property to the original owners, among other things (Leviticus 25:8–55).

Suffice it to say that joy—and sharing joy—is a key part of who our God is.

Bottom Line: God is *full* of joy!

For further study: Job 8:21; Psalms 16:11; 19:8; Proverbs 8:30–32; Isaiah 62:5; Zephaniah 3:17; John 17:13; Acts 13:52; Romans 15:13; Galatians 5:22

Related to: Good, Love

JUST

MORAL RELATIVE DOES

"The LORD reigns forever, executing judgment from his throne. He will judge the world with justice and rule the nations with fairness."

PSALM 9:7–8

"He has set a day for judging the world with justice by the man he has appointed, and he proved to everyone who this is by raising him from the dead."

ACTS 17:31

When we say that God is just, we mean that he always does what is right. We also mean that *whatever he does is right because he does it*; we never imply that he adheres to some standard of rightness outside of himself. God alone defines what is just and right, meaning his standard for justice is *the* standard, eternally right and unchanging. Human justice, by contrast, changes from culture to culture and generation to generation and is subject to sinful corruptions that are absent in God.

Interestingly, although God is always just, he is not always *fair*—at least not according to our notions of fairness. His merciful nature frequently outweighs his righteous judgment, which certainly isn't fair but works in our favor. And his frequent generosity, which is just, may not always seem fair to us. For instance, in the parables of the prodigal son (Luke 15:11–32) and the workers in the vineyard (Matthew 20:1–16), the figure symbolizing God generously gives blessings to those who are undeserving.

Here is the hard part of the justness of God: It means he will punish wrongdoing, and that punishment can be severe, both in this life and in the life after death. King David experienced God's justice personally, and it was devastating (2 Samuel 12:1–23; 24:10–25). After Israel and Judah spent generations worshiping idols in detestable ways, God finally enacted justice on both nations by sending foreign powers to conquer them (2 Kings 17:1–23; 24:1–4; 24:18–25:21). The New Testament also records several instances of God's judgment (Acts 5:1–11; 12:20–23; 1 Corinthians 11:29–30; Revelation 2:20–23).

The ultimate example of God giving out justice for wrongdoing is hell, which comes after his judgment in the afterlife. Scripture teaches that hell was first created "for the devil and his demons" (Matthew 25:41), but it will also be a place of punishment for those who follow the devil instead of God (Matthew 10:28; Hebrews 10:26–27). It is tragedy to avoid.

In spite of God's absolute right—and full ability—to justly punish wrongdoing, John 3:16 reveals that he will provide mercy if we ask: "This is how God loved the world: He gave his one and only Son, so that everyone who believes in him will not perish but have eternal life."

Bottom Line: God is just. He will punish your sin, but his preference is to show you his mercy, which is found in Jesus.

For further study: Genesis 18:23–26; Deuteronomy 32:4; Job 37:23–24; Psalms 7:17; 51:4; 75:7; John 5:26–30; Romans 2:1–10; Galatians 6:7; Hebrews 1:8–9

Related to: Faithful, Good, Jealous, Mercy, Redeemer, Righteous, Truth, Wrath

LOVE

MORAL

RELATIVE

IS

DOES

"God showed his great love for us by sending Christ to die for us while we were still sinners."

Romans 5:8

"God is love."

1 John 4:8

The unrivaled love of God is *the* central theme of the entire Bible. So it should be easy to explain it completely in the next few paragraphs, right? Of course not, but we can celebrate some of the highlights!

The apostle John taught us this two thousand years ago: *God is love*. In other words, God's essential being is what has created and maintains the thing we call *love*; without him, that word has no meaning or being at all.

Here's a sampling of what Scripture teaches us about this awe-inspiring love of God:

- God's love is his unconditional choice alone, and we can do nothing to earn or deserve it (Deuteronomy 7:7–8; Romans 5:8).
- God's love is the means by which we can be rescued from sin (Ephesians 2:4–5; Titus 3:4–5).

- God's love is unshakable, unbreakable, and impenetrable (Romans 8:35–39).
- God's love is forever, unchanging, and unfailing (Psalms 103:17; 143:8; Jeremiah 31:3; John 1:14, 17).
- God's Holy Spirit fills us with his love (Romans 5:5; Galatians 5:22).
- God's love is the supreme work of his Holy Spirit in our lives (1 Corinthians 13:13).
- God's love makes us his adopted children (1 John 3:1).

There is more, of course, but that is enough as we end this section by echoing Paul's prayer in Ephesians 3:18–19.

> May you have the power to understand, as all God's people should, how wide, how long, how high, and how deep his love is. May you experience the love of Christ, though it is too great to understand fully.

Bottom Line: God is love, possesses love, gives love, and you are the object of that incredible love.

For further study: 1 Chronicles 16:34; Psalms 63:3; 86:5; Lamentations 3:22–23; John 3:16; 1 Corinthians 13:4–7; Ephesians 1:4–5; 1 John 4:7–19

Related to: Compassion, Father, Mercy

MERCY

MORAL

RELATIVE

DOES

"Great is his faithfulness; his mercies begin afresh each morning."

LAMENTATIONS 3:23

"Mercy triumphs over judgment."

JAMES 2:13 NIV

Mercy in Scripture is always an *action*; it's an intervention to alleviate suffering, not just a feeling of sympathy. As such, it's a deliberate, outward act of God's compassion, love, and kindness. When we say that God possesses mercy, we declare that God is continually *acting out love toward those in misery*, whether or not they deserve it.

The Old Testament uses several Hebrew words for this mercy, but the most common is *hesed,* which means "favor, goodness, or kindness." The Greek word is *eleos* which connotes both mercy and tenderhearted pity for a suffering person. This is the context for understanding the stunning sacrifice of Jesus on the cross and his victorious resurrection, which won for us the permanent dismissal of the penalty of sin. As Peter said, "It is by his great mercy that we have been born again, because God raised Jesus Christ from the dead" (1 Peter 1:3).

Descriptions of God's great mercy are littered like gems throughout Scripture, but perhaps one example would be good to mention here: Second Chronicles 33:1–20 records a summary of the reign of the evil king Manasseh. This man built pagan shrines and worshiped idols, even inside the temple of the Lord. He practiced witchcraft and spiritism and sacrificed his own children as burnt offerings to false gods. For half a century he passionately led the people of Judah away from God and into perverse idol worship. Finally, God sent the Assyrian army to take him captive: "They put a ring through his nose, bound him in bronze chains, and led him away" (verse 11). While in "deep distress" (verse 12), Manasseh begged God for mercy, and God answered that evil man's prayer! Scripture tells us that "the Lord brought Manasseh back to Jerusalem and to his kingdom. Then Manasseh finally realized that the Lord alone is God" (verse 13). Amen!

Bottom Line: "Mercy triumphs over judgment" (James 2:13 NIV).

For further study: Exodus 34:6; Deuteronomy 4:31; 1 Samuel 9:15–17; Psalm 51:1; 136:1; Mark 10:46–52; Luke 18:9–14; Romans 11:30–31; Philippians 2:25–27

Related to: Compassion, Grace, Just, Love, Patient, Redeemer, Righteous

OMNIPOTENT

ABSOLUTE DOES

"When Abram was ninety-nine years old, the LORD appeared to him and said, 'I am El-Shaddai—God Almighty.'"

GENESIS 17:1

"With God everything is possible."

MATTHEW 19:26

"God Almighty!"

That's literally what it means to say that God is omnipotent. The Hebrew *El-Shaddai* (Genesis 17:1) and the Greek *Theos Pantokrator* (Revelation 4:8) both translate the same: "God Almighty." Today we'd more commonly say "God is all powerful." (The prefix "omni" means "all," which is why it's used here and in other descriptions of God's specific attributes.)

The simplest definition of *omnipotent* is the same one that Jesus gave in Matthew 19:26, "With God everything is possible." This power of God means he can accomplish anything he chooses, including the creation of the universe, the formation of your invisible soul, the orchestration of history, and any miraculous act he wants. In trying to grasp this concept, it can be very easy to think that God's limitless power means that he cannot be limited. Instead, we need to understand Jesus's definition of omnipotence in this way:

God's power always succeeds—never fails.

Saying that nothing is impossible for God means that God cannot do anything that's inconsistent with his character or being. For instance, God cannot sin. Because he is the definition of holiness (1 Peter 1:15–16), anything he does is holy—therefore, he can never sin (Deuteronomy 32:4; 1 Peter 2:22). Likewise, God cannot lie (Titus 1:2) or break a promise (Numbers 23:19). God can't stop loving (Psalm 103:17; Romans 8:38–39) or stop existing (1 Chronicles 16:36). And no, he cannot create a rock so heavy that he can't lift it—because God cannot fail.

So when considering the omnipotence of God, we must avoid over thinking it and instead realize that it simply means what it says: *God alone has full power to accomplish anything he chooses to do.* With him, nothing is too hard, no obstacle immovable, no force unstoppable. Nothing is impossible for God.

Bottom Line: As Jesus said, "With God everything is possible" (Matthew 19:26).

For further study: Genesis 18:14; Job 42:1–2; Psalms 93:3–4; 135:5–6; Isaiah 14:24, 27; Mark 14:36; Luke 1:37; Romans 4:20–21; Ephesians 1:19–21; Revelation 19:6

Related to: Autonomy, Creator, Immanent, Infinite, Omnipresent, Omniscient, Peace, Sovereign

OMNIPRESENT

"I can never escape from your Spirit! I can never get away from your presence! If I go up to heaven, you are there; if I go down to the grave, you are there. If I ride the wings of the morning, if I dwell by the farthest oceans, even there your hand will guide me, and your strength will support me. I could ask the darkness to hide me and the light around me to become night— but even in darkness I cannot hide from you."

PSALM 139:7–12

"'Can anyone hide from me in a secret place? Am I not everywhere in all the heavens and earth?' says the LORD."

JEREMIAH 23:24

Paul taught that in Christ all people "live and move and have our being" (Acts 17:28 NIV), and in him "all things hold together" (Colossians 1:17 NIV). How is all this possible? Only because God is omnipresent—that is, *he is present everywhere all at once*. The simple fact is that anything in existence can only exist because God exists where that thing exists. (How was that for overemphasizing the word *exist* in a single sentence?)

Some think this means that *only a part* of God is present in all places, but that's a serious error coming from our finite human understanding. Because we can only exist in one place at a time, we assume that God must parcel parts of himself out in order for him to be everywhere at once. The reality, though, is that God is infinite and therefore infinitely present in his totality in every place (1 Kings 8:27).

Although God is present everywhere, that doesn't mean he must perform the same actions in every place. His omnipresence gives him the ability to act in many various ways, in many various places, all at the same time.

"God can be present to punish, sustain, or bless," writes theologian Wayne Grudem.[13] For example, Amos 9 reveals God's all-reaching presence with a warning of judgment, Colossians 1:17 discusses his sustaining presence, and Psalm 16:11 rejoices in the blessing of God's presence.

Bottom Line: God is always present with you.

For further study: Psalm 145:3, 18; Proverbs 15:3; Isaiah 66:1; Jeremiah 23:23–24; Amos 9:1–4; Matthew 28:20; Acts 17:24

Related to: Immanent, Omnipotent, Omniscient

OMNISCIENT

ABSOLUTE

DOES

"You see me when I travel and when I rest at home. You know everything I do. You know what I am going to say even before I say it, LORD."

PSALM 139:3–4

"Nothing in all creation is hidden from God. Everything is naked and exposed before his eyes, and he is the one to whom we are accountable."

HEBREWS 4:13

To say that God is omniscient is to declare that he is *all-knowing*. That sounds simple at first glance, but it carries some complex implications. Consider the following:

- God knows himself completely and infinitely; the things which we struggle to grasp and can only imagine about God, he knows, down to the minutest detail (Romans 11:33–34; 1 Corinthians 2:11).
- God knows all of the facts about every single thing (Hebrews 4:13; 1 John 3:20).
- God knows everything about the past and the future (Isaiah 46:9–10).

- God knows everything about you, down to the smallest detail (Matthew 6:8; 10:30).
- God knows everything that is possible (including the what-ifs of life), even when they are not actual (1 Samuel 23:11–13; Matthew 11:21–23).

At the same time, God in his eternal infiniteness knows everything without having to recall anything. He is able to hold all knowledge at the same time, without the need for short-term or long-term memory. Theologian Wayne Grudem explains, "God is always fully aware of everything. If he should wish to tell us the number of grains of sand on the seashore or the number stars in the sky, he would not have to count them.... He always knows all things at once."[14] And because his limitless knowledge is eternal and unchanging, God never learns anything new. For him alone Ecclesiastes 1:9 (NIV) is literally true: "There is nothing new under the sun."

God's limitless knowledge works in conjunction with his infinite wisdom and understanding (Job 12:13).

Bottom Line: God is never stumped by your problems—or your questions.

For further study: Genesis 6:5; Job 37:14–18; Psalm 147:4; Isaiah 42:9; Matthew 6:8; 10:29–31; Acts 1:24; 1 John 3:20

Related to: Omnipotent, Omnipresent, Wise

PATIENT

MORAL RELATIVE DOES

"The LORD is compassionate and merciful, slow to get angry and filled with unfailing love."

PSALM 103:8

"The Lord isn't really being slow about his promise, as some people think. No, he is being patient for your sake. He does not want anyone to be destroyed, but wants everyone to repent."

2 PETER 3:9

In the Bible, God's patience—also translated as "long-suffering" and "slow to get angry"—is often paired with his mercy or compassion, as in Psalm 103:8 above or as in Exodus 34:6. The Hebrew word is *arek*, which means literally "long," and typically describes God's restraint in the face of abuse or opposition. The Greek word is *makrothymia* (as in 2 Peter 3:9 above). While it carries much the same meaning as *arek*, it adds the idea of endurance or "a long holding out of the mind" before God enacts judgment in response to sin.[15]

Examples of God's patience in Scripture almost always deal with his proactive decision to delay punishment in order to give time for people to repent. The book of Jonah shows this kind of long-suffering purpose in action. Jonah tells the Ninevites to repent or their city will be destroyed. Because God is patient with them, the people of Nineveh actually do repent and ask for mercy, which God grants.

Paul considered himself to be a living example of God's patience. A devout Pharisee, he said of himself, "I was so zealous that I harshly persecuted the church" (Philippians 3:6). But instead of punishing him, Jesus miraculously met him on the road to Damascus and led him to repent (Acts 9:1–19). Of that moment, Paul later wrote, "God had mercy on me so that Christ Jesus could use me as a prime example of his great patience with even the worst sinners" (1 Timothy 1:16).

You too are a living example of God's patience. Now what will you do with that?

Bottom Line: God waits patiently for you to turn to him.

For further study: Numbers 14:18; Nehemiah 9:16–22; Psalm 78:38; Romans 2:4; Galatians 5:22; 1 Peter 3:20; 2 Peter 3:15

Related to: Compassion, Faithful, Father, Mercy

PEACE

MORAL RELATIVE DOES

"Gideon built an altar to the* LORD *there and named it Yahweh-Shalom (which means 'the* LORD *is peace')."

JUDGES 6:24

"[God] himself is our peace."

EPHESIANS 2:14 NIV

Peace, in the Western world, is most often understood as the absence of conflict. That's certainly a crucial aspect of peace, but it is only the beginning of what the ancient Hebrews understood by it. The Old Testament word for peace is *shalom*, and New Testament writers used the Greek word *eirene*. The peace that these words describe encompasses "wholeness, unity, and harmony—something that is complete and sound ... prosperity, health, and fulfillment."[16]

This fuller definition is how we should understand peace as an attribute of God—that he possesses within himself the perfection of wholeness, unity, and harmony, as well as the absence of any kind of conflict. As Paul taught, "God is not a God of disorder but of peace" (1 Corinthians 14:33). With that in mind, it's interesting to see how God's presence alone is enough to bestow peace on his people.

Paul wrote to the Colossian believers, encouraging them to "let the peace that comes from Christ rule in your hearts" (Colossians 3:15) as way to overcome cultural and relational differences and create unity in their church. King David faced many dangers and struggles. In the midst of turmoil, he found an unnatural inner peace rooted in God's nearness to him: "In peace I will lie down and sleep, for you alone, O LORD, will keep me safe" (Psalm 4:8). Isaiah prophesied about the future messianic Prince of Peace and declared that when he arrives, "This righteousness will bring peace. Yes, it will bring quietness and confidence forever. My people will live in safety, quietly at home. They will be at rest" (Isaiah 32:17–18). We know this promised Messiah is Jesus.

From this we understand that God is not passively enfolded by peace but that in his omnipotence, he is the proactive embodiment of peace.

Bottom Line: The only place you can find true peace is in God, because he alone is *Yahweh-Shalom*.

For further study: Psalm 119:165; Isaiah 26:3; Matthew 5:9; John 14:27; 16:33; Romans 8:6; 16:20; Philippians 4:6–7

Related to: Omnipotent

PERFECT

MORAL

RELATIVE

IS

"God's way is perfect."

PSALM 18:30

"But you are to be perfect, even as your Father in heaven is perfect."

MATTHEW 5:48

Today it seems unremarkable to say God is perfect, but in the ancient world that was simply unheard of—gods, as everyone knew, were full of greed and deceit. For example, Zeus cheated on his wife uncountable times, rape was commonly practiced by the gods, and it was thought that Baal committed incest with his sister, Anath. Other tales spoke of so-called gods starting petty wars, stealing from each other, lying without any reservation, and so on. So when the newly freed Hebrews declared of God, "He is the Rock; his deeds are perfect. Everything he does is just and fair" (Deuteronomy 32:4), it was huge departure from the norm.

There are several nuances of meaning at play when Scripture says that God is perfect.

First and most obvious is the idea that God is morally flawless and entirely without sin (Job 34:12; 1 Peter 2:22).

In this sense, when we speak of God being holy, we can say with authority that he is *perfectly* holy.

Second, when Scripture speaks of God's perfection, it means that he is *whole* and *complete* (Acts 17:24–25). No thing can be added to or taken from his being, and he exists eternally without the need to grow or learn or "get better" (1 Corinthians 2:16). This concept includes what some theologians call the simplicity of God: "God is not the sum total of his attributes but is simultaneously everything that all of the attributes reveal."[17] He is complete and whole—*perfect*—all by himself.

Finally, the perfection of God refers to something of the highest standard—one that is above all else (Psalm 97:9; Philippians 2:9–11)—and in that way it applies to every attribute in this book. For instance, God is not only good, he is perfectly good. God possesses perfect beauty, he acts with perfect justice, and he alone loves perfectly—in ways that are holy, complete, and of the highest standard.

Bottom Line: "Every good and perfect gift" comes from God (James 1:17 NIV), because he alone is the eternal standard of perfection.

For further study: 2 Samuel 22:31, 33; Job 37:16; Psalms 19:7; 27:4; 119:138; Hebrews 2:10; 5:9

Related to: Beauty, Holy

REDEEMER

MORAL RELATIVE DOES

"As for me, I know that my Redeemer lives, and he will stand upon the earth at last."

Job 19:25

"Jesus gave his life for our sins, just as God our Father planned, in order to rescue us from this evil world in which we live."

Galatians 1:4

It is God's nature to redeem—that is, to rescue. This was first seen in the earliest moments of history, when "the Lord God made clothing from animal skins for Adam and his wife" (Genesis 3:21) before sending them out of Eden—yet not out of his presence. Then his rescuing nature was shown full-blown in miraculous power when he delivered the people of Israel out from slavery in Egypt.

As a biblical concept, then, redemption is always a costly rescue from an impossible situation by One who freely helps the helpless.

In the Old Testament, the term *redeemer* usually refers to God, although on occasion it can refer to a human (Ruth 4:1–12). God's rescue is characterized by both physical redemption (Jeremiah 31:11; 50:33–34) and spiritual forgiveness of sin (Psalm 130:7–8). In the New Testament, God's redemptive work is often spiritual—the forgiveness of sin through the sacrifice of Jesus Christ on the cross—though it does include the redemption of the body at Christ's return (Romans 3:24; 8:23; Galatians 1:4).

God's redemptive nature is centered in his love and compassion and is accomplished by his omnipotence (Isaiah 45:22–23). In the New Testament's spiritual sense, his active rescue from the penalty of sin is always available to us because of Jesus (Hebrews 4:14–16). In the physical sense, such as oppressive life situations or disability and illness, God may delay his redemptive work, as a means of carrying out his purpose in the midst of suffering (Romans 8:18–28). In all situations, though, this truth still remains: *It is God's nature to redeem.*

Bottom Line: Because your Redeemer lives, he will rescue you.

For further study: Exodus 6:6; Psalm 78:35; Mark 10:45; Galatians 3:13–14; Ephesians 1:7; Colossians 1:13; Titus 2:14; 1 Peter 1:18–19

Related to: Compassion, Just, Love, Mercy, Omnipotent

RIGHTEOUS

MORAL RELATIVE DOES

"The Lord is righteous in everything he does; he is filled with kindness."

Psalm 145:17

"Since we know that Christ is righteous, we also know that all who do what is right are God's children."

1 John 2:29

What does *righteous* mean exactly? In the Bible, it often refers to people acting justly, acting in obedience to God, and being in right relationship with God and others. When applied to God, it takes on a broader meaning.

When the Bible talks about God being righteous, it means that whatever God does is always right—even when we might not understand his actions or if we disagree with what he does. This is because God himself is the standard of righteousness (Deuteronomy 32:4; Isaiah 45:19). There is no other true measure of right and wrong, so regardless of what we might think, anything he chooses to do is the right thing to do.

God's righteousness is seen most clearly in his acts of justice and mercy. He is right when he punishes sin, and he is also right when he rewards obedience to his commands. At the same time, when he chooses mercy instead of punishment, that's also right.

So even though God always does what is right, the reason it's righteous is simply because God has done it. That's what it means to say that God is righteous.

Bottom Line: God is always right, whether you agree with him or not.

For further study: Genesis 18:25; Psalms 19:8; 71:19; Isaiah 45:24; Daniel 9:7–14; John 16:8–10; 17:25; Romans 2:5; 3:5; 6:16; 2 Peter 3:13; Revelation 15:4; 19:11

Related to: Glory, Holy, Jealous, Just, Mercy, Truth, Wrath

SELF-EXISTENT

ABSOLUTE

IS

"Before the mountains were born, before you gave birth to the earth and the world, from beginning to end, you are God."

Psalm 90:2

"Christ is the visible image of the invisible God. He existed before anything was created and is supreme over all creation."

Colossians 1:15

In all of everything, only one thing is uncreated: God.

God alone has no beginning or end, no point of origin, no cause or effect, zero dependence on anything or anyone but himself. He exists simply because he is. Or as he communicated to Moses and the ancient Israelites, God is "I am" (Exodus 3:14), and as Jesus explained in John 5:26, "The Father has life in himself, and he has granted that same life-giving power to his Son."

This self-existent attribute of God is what theologians call aseity, and it means literally "from-himself-ness."[18] That's an unfamiliar word to most of us, but it just means that God depends only on himself—always. We need air, food, shelter, and clothing to exist. God needs none of that or anything else. He lives eternally, with full power to do whatever he wants whenever he wants, simply because he is God (Psalm 50:10–12; Acts 17:24–25). That's what we mean when we say that God is self-existent.

Because God is completely independent in his uncreated being, all created things (humans, planets, atoms, etc.) are completely dependent on him for their existence. As Jesus famously declared, "Apart from me you can do nothing" (John 15:5).

Bottom Line: God exists. He always has, and he always will.

For further study: Isaiah 40:28; John 8:58; Colossians 1:17; 1 Timothy 1:17; Hebrews 13:8; Revelation 1:8

Related to: Autonomy, Eternal, Infinite, Trinity

SOVEREIGN

ABSOLUTE

MORAL

NATURAL

DOES

"How great you are, O Sovereign LORD! There is no one like you. We have never even heard of another God like you!"

2 SAMUEL 7:22

"There is one Lord, one faith, one baptism, one God and Father of all, who is over all, in all, and living through all."

EPHESIANS 4:5–6

When we think about God's sovereignty, the idea of royalty immediately comes to mind. This isn't a bad connection, as Scripture does frequently speak of God in kingly terms (Psalm 95:3, Isaiah 6:1; Revelation 15:3). That image is certainly helpful in understanding how God is sovereign, but it tells only part of the story.

The fuller understanding of God's sovereignty speaks about his *freedom, authority,* and *ability* as the Almighty.

First, God has complete *freedom* to choose his own will in any situation (Psalm 115:3). He's not compelled by anything or anyone else, not constrained by any factor other than his own preference. In that sense, he's fully sovereign over himself, entirely free to be self-directed in a way that's impossible for us.

Second, by virtue of who he is, God has full *authority* to do what he pleases. This is where the image of a heavenly King is helpful, because it uses a human figure immediately understood as having authority. Even King Hezekiah prayed to the ultimate King, saying, "O Lord, God of Israel, you are enthroned between the mighty cherubim! You alone are God of all the kingdoms of the earth" (2 Kings 19:15).

And finally, God has absolute, unhindered *ability* to accomplish anything he chooses to do (Job 42:1–2; Matthew 19:26). His kingship does not mean he is a powerless figurehead but rather the omnipotent Sovereign able to exercise his freedom of choice and authority in any time, place, and situation he chooses.

Bottom Line: God has full freedom, authority, and ability to accomplish whatever he intends.

For further study: 1 Samuel 2:6; 2 Samuel 7:28; Psalm 103:19; Daniel 4:34–35; John 18:36; Acts 4:24–28; 1 Timothy 1:17; Revelation 17:14; 19:11–16

Related to: Autonomy, Omnipotent

SPIRIT

RELATIVE IS

"[God] is not human."

NUMBERS 23:19

"God is Spirit, so those who worship him must worship in spirit and in truth."

JOHN 4:24

God is Spirit, meaning he exists in our world in a way that we can't see or experience with our five senses—unless he chooses to reveal himself to us in some way.

Since God is pure Spirit, he's not subject to any limitations of physical being. For instance, he is everywhere at once, exempt from illness or decay, ungendered, and eternal.

It's also important to recognize that God is not described as *a* spirit, as that would imply, not only that he's simply one of many, but also that he had been created. Instead, God is revealed to be Spirit, which indicates a uniqueness and an ultimate supremacy of being, something consistent with other descriptions of God in Scripture (1 Timothy 6:15–16).

The Greek word for Spirit in John 4:24 (above) is *pneuma*, which also signifies "breath" or "wind." In this sense, we also see the Spirit nature of God as the sole originator of life. For instance, when Genesis 2:7 reports that God "breathed the breath of life into the man's nostrils, and the man became a living person," the understanding is that God's Spirit brought Adam to life. This is underscored in Jesus's words: "The Spirit gives life; the flesh counts for nothing" (John 6:63 NIV).

Finally, the ancient Hebrews believed that the immaterial Spirit nature of God was at least part of the reasoning behind the second commandment's prohibition against making carved images, which led to idol worship (Exodus 20:4–5). After all, how could any object made by humans represent the true, unseen, invisible, Spirit of God?

Bottom Line: God is not human; he is pure Spirit and does not share any human limitation and weakness.

For further study: Genesis 1:1–2; Deuteronomy 4:15–18; 1 Kings 8:27; John 1:18; 2 Corinthians 3:17; 1 John 4:12

Related to: Infinite, Invisible, Trinity, Ungendered

TRINITY

"Then God said, 'Let us make human beings in our image, to be like us.'"

GENESIS 1:26

"The Holy Spirit, in bodily form, descended on [Jesus] like a dove. And a voice from heaven said, "You are my dearly loved Son, and you bring me great joy""

LUKE 3:22

The basic concept of the Trinity is that *God is three-in-one.* That is, while there is only one God, he exists eternally in three persons. In the Bible,

- the Father is called God (2 Thessalonians 1:2);
- the Son (Jesus) is called God (John 1:1–5; 10:30–33; 20:28; Hebrews 1:8; Philippians 2:9–11); and
- the Holy Spirit is called God (Acts 5:3–4).

God is one substance but three persons in relationship. There are more than sixty passages in the Bible that mention the three persons together.

The truth that the three persons are one God has caused some distorted thinking over the centuries. Modalism tried to explain God as one person playing three different roles, like a woman who is a wife, mother, and sister. That helped maintain the unity of God as one but couldn't account for the clear plurality of God indicated in Scripture. Partialism said that God is made up of three parts, like an egg that has yolk, white, and shell. That preserved a trinity, but neglected unity, making each person of the Trinity only one-third of God. And Arianism declared that God the Father was God, and Jesus and the Holy Spirit were his exalted creations. This failed to explain either God's unity or his trinity of being.

Because we're limited by our human nature, none of us will fully understand the spiritual reality of the Trinity of God. The best explanation for the Trinity, therefore, is to make no explanation at all. Knowing that our understanding is incomplete, we can accept by faith that the Bible is true when it speaks of God in three persons who is at the same time always one, single, true God.

Bottom Line: You may not fully understand it, but what the Scriptures describe is true: God is one *and at the same time* he is three persons.

For further study: Genesis 3:22; 11:7; Isaiah 6:8; 48:16; Matthew 28:19; 1 Corinthians 12:4–5; 2 Corinthians 13:14; 1 Peter 1:2

Related to: Invisible, Self-Existent, Spirit

TRUTH

MORAL RELATIVE DOES

"The sum of your word is truth, and every one of your righteous rules endures forever."

Psalm 119:160 ESV

"Jesus told him, 'I am the way, the truth, and the life. No one can come to the Father except through me.'"

John 14:6

When we say that God possesses truth, we mean that "God represents things as they really are. Whether speaking of himself or part of his creation, what God says is accurate."[19] Because of that, everything God says or does is true—he alone is the pure standard for truth.

Scripture explicitly applies truth to all three persons of the Trinity. For instance, Psalm 31:5 calls Father God *emet el* "God of truth," often translated as "faithful God." Jesus is "the way, the truth, and the life" (John 14:6), and the Holy Spirit is identified as "the Spirit of truth" (John 15:26).

God's truth extends to his Scripture (2 Timothy 2:15) and to the law he gave through Moses (Psalm 19:9–10). Most importantly, Jesus promised that knowing God's "truth will set you free" (John 8:32). This is a reference to both emotional and spiritual freedom as well as to eternal life in God's kingdom yet to come.

The knowledge that God possesses eternal truth ought to be both freeing and humbling for us. Freeing because through his guidance, we can learn to see the world as it really is—both the physical, seen world, and the spiritual, unseen world. Humbling, because we know that "now we see through a glass, darkly" (1 Corinthians 13:12 KJV), so we must be careful not to assume that we have a complete understanding of all of God's truth. May we always remember to handle God's truth with humility in our daily lives.

Bottom Line: God is true, speaks true, and acts true. He alone is the substance of truth.

For further study: 1 Samuel 15:29; Psalm 18:30; Proverbs 30:5; Isaiah 65:16; John 14:16–17; 17:17; Romans 3:4; Hebrews 6:18

Related to: Holy, Just, Righteous, Wise

UNGENDERED

ABSOLUTE IS

"God created human beings in his own image. In the image of God he created them; male and female he created them."

GENESIS 1:27

"All who have been united with Christ in baptism have put on Christ, like putting on new clothes. There is no longer Jew or Gentile, slave or free, male and female. For you are all one in Christ Jesus."

GALATIANS 3:27–28

First, it's important to understand that *only God is ungendered*—it's one of his absolute attributes and is not shared with us. Human physicality is defined by individual genders that reflect God's image; but God, who is not physical but "is Spirit" (John 4:24), is not defined that way.

That said, ungendered God is not simply *both* male and female. Nor is God *only* female or *only* male. A better understanding is that *God, who is Spirit, transcends human gender* in a mysterious way that completely encompasses the perfections of male and female uniqueness.

Scripture is clear on this doctrine, using both male and female terms in multiple descriptions of God. For instance, at creation we're told that God created humanity “in the image of God … male and female” (Genesis 1:27). God refers to himself as “God who gave you birth” (Deuteronomy 32:18, NIV) and says, “like a woman in childbirth, I cry out, I gasp and pant” (Isaiah 42:14, NIV). God’s wisdom is personified as female in the book of Proverbs. Jesus also used both masculine and feminine images for God; for example, in his parables of lost things, he symbolized God both as a woman who lost a coin and a father who lost a son (Luke 15:8–32). Paul declared unequivocally that being in Christ meant “there is no longer … male and female” (Galatians 3:28).

At the same time, it’s impossible to dismiss the overwhelming application of the masculine gender to God throughout Scripture. Pronouns for God, in both the Old and New Testaments, are almost always masculine. God is repeatedly described as Father (Malachi 2:10; Matthew 6:9) but never Mother. Jesus became a physical man (Luke 2:4–7) and he retained that masculinity after his resurrection (Acts 13:34). Even the Holy Spirit is called “he” (John 15:26).

So we must understand that even though we refer to God as “he,” as is clearly indicated in the Bible, that doesn’t mean we must at the same time remove or ignore the biblical truth that God is ungendered. God created man and woman as physical beings, but because he is limitless Spirit, he is uniquely and mysteriously transcendent above any physical limitation of male or female.

Bottom Line: God transcends gender.

For further study: Numbers 23:19; Proverbs 3:13–19; Isaiah 66:13; Hosea 13:8; Matthew 23:37

Related to: Infinite, Spirit

WISE

MORAL

RELATIVE

IS

"God is so wise and so mighty. Who has ever challenged him successfully?"

Job 9:4

"To the only wise God be glory forevermore through Jesus Christ! Amen."

Romans 16:27 ESV

Not only does God know all things, but he is also *all-wise*—meaning that he alone understands how to best use every scrap of his infinite knowledge to achieve the highest goal. Speaking of Jesus, Paul summarized this truth in Colossians 2:3: "In him lie hidden all the treasures of wisdom and knowledge."

The wisdom of God is immediately seen when we take a glimpse into the science of creation (Psalm 104:24; Proverbs 3:19). Humanity still can't duplicate or even understand all the infinite, interconnected miracles required to establish life, growth, and health. At best, we can study snippets of what God has done, propose theories, and test hypotheses. But life itself? Only God is wise enough to actually make that happen.

Additionally, the prophet Isaiah recorded God saying, "My thoughts are nothing like your thoughts.... And my ways are far beyond anything you could imagine. For just as the heavens are higher than the earth, so my ways are higher than your ways and my thoughts higher than your thoughts" (Isaiah 55:8–9). This is significant because even though God obviously possesses all wisdom, he does not *hoard* it. In fact, throughout Scripture he invites us to ask him to share his wisdom with us—and he promises to give it.

Proverbs 2:3–6 tells us, "Cry out for insight, and ask for understanding. Search for them as you would for silver; seek them like hidden treasures.... For the LORD grants wisdom! From his mouth come knowledge and understanding." James, the half-brother of Jesus, echoed that Old Testament advice when he wrote, "If you need wisdom, ask our generous God, and he will give it to you. He will not rebuke you for asking" (James 1:5).

Most importantly, the limitless wisdom of God is an anchor for our faith in him. Life is—and always will be—difficult. Yet in every situation and sorrow and unanswered prayer, we can trust that "God causes everything to work together for the good of those who love God and are called according to his purpose for them" (Romans 8:28). How can we trust that promise? Because we know our God is wise.

Bottom Line: God is *all-wise,* and he's willing to share his wisdom with you.

For further study: 1 Kings 3:10–12; Job 12:13, 16; Jeremiah 10:12; Daniel 2:20–23; Romans 11:33; 1 Corinthians 1:20–25; Colossians 1:9–10

Related to: Omniscient, Truth

WRATH

MORAL

RELATIVE

DOES

"When I sharpen my flashing sword and begin to carry out justice, I will take revenge on my enemies and repay those who reject me. I will make my arrows drunk with blood, and my sword will devour flesh."

DEUTERONOMY 32:41–42

"He will pour out his anger and wrath on those who live for themselves, who refuse to obey the truth and instead live lives of wickedness."

ROMANS 2:8

It can be quite startling—and dismaying—to think of God as wrathful. Reading about his compassion and wrath in the same book may lead you to think you're reading about two different versions of God. But we are not to defend the uncomfortable aspects of our Creator but to explore *what God has disclosed about himself* in the Bible. And whether we like it or not, our God who is love (1 John 4:8) has also shown himself to be wrathful.

The wrath of God is rooted in his holiness, jealousy, and righteous justice. With that in mind, we can define God's wrath as *his anger in response to a sinful offense, which arouses his jealousy and requires his just punishment.*

The Bible is full of examples of this kind of wrath. For example, God's anger did not allow the Israelites to enter the promised land for forty years (Hebrews 3:7–11) and their complaining prompted him to respond with deadly fire (Numbers 11:1–3). God's wrath over unchecked idolatry prompted him to destroy both the kingdoms of Israel and of Judah (2 Kings 17:5–18; 24–25). Other events that provoked God's wrath include failure to obey God's word or his prophets (Zechariah 7:12); refusal to worship God (2 Chronicles 29:6–8); and adultery and murderous deceit (2 Samuel 12:1–22). In the future, God will display his wrath on those who showed no regard for those in need (Matthew 25:31–46).

Just a few of the ways that Scripture describes his wrath are blazing fire (Leviticus 10:1–2); plagues (Amos 4:10); eternal destruction (2 Thessalonians 1:9); fearsome vengeance (Hebrews 10:30–31), and the many terrors recorded in the book of Revelation.

So what are we to do?

First, we must understand that *God is patient* and has frequently restrained his righteous anger—so much so that he's the ultimate biblical example of one who is "slow to anger" (Exodus 34:6; Psalm 78:38; Romans 9:22–23).

Second and even better: *Jesus has made the way for us to escape God's wrath*—despite our many sinful offenses against God. This was accomplished through his life, death, and resurrection. Consider what Paul wrote in

1 Thessalonians 5:9: "God chose to save us through our Lord Jesus Christ, not to pour out his anger on us" (Romans 8:1–2; Ephesians 2:2–5).

While wrath is frightening, it is clearly an attribute of God for which he makes no apology. We would be wise to accept his gracious provision in Christ and thus avoid his awful anger.

Bottom Line: God's wrath is a reality, but Jesus has made the way for you to escape that horror.

For further study: Deuteronomy 9:7–8; Psalms 7:11; 94:1–10; John 11:33–38; Romans 1:18; 3:25–26; 1 Thessalonians 1:10; 5:9–11; 2 Peter 3:10–12; Revelation 6:9–17; 19:11–16

Related to: Holy, Jealous, Just, Righteous

CONCLUSION

Thank you for journeying through this brief exploration of God's amazing attributes as revealed in the Bible. You have learned about his nature, his character, his actions, his priorities, and his preferences. In doing so, you've unveiled something of who he is and what he does. That's no small feat—congratulations!

Now what will you do with all that you've learned?

First, remember that there's more to learn. Entire books could be (and in many cases have been) written on each one of the attributes covered here. So don't let your study of God stop with the last page of this book. You can find more helpful resources at your local Christian bookstore and the Rose Publishing website: rose-publishing.com.

Second, talk about God with others. Some like to use Made Easy books as the basis for a Bible study group, while others prefer reading and discussing a book like this over coffee with a friend. You might share this book with your family, neighbors, and even with non-Christians. Talking about what you've read will help you work through questions you might still have, decide if you agree or disagree with something, and send you directly to the Bible where you can build on and clarify the knowledge you've gained.

Finally, think about the ways you will respond to God with this new understanding of who he is. How will this affect the way you pray? The way you worship and read Scripture? The things you do when you feel like God's not listening—or when you're overwhelmed with joy by his obvious activity in your life? The way you respond is yours alone. You decide what you should or shouldn't do, what you can and can't do—what you *want* to do and what you don't. So take some time to think about it, talk it over with God, and let your new understanding of him change who you become in the days, months, and years ahead.

Again, thank you for taking time to simply look at God with an unwavering gaze. May God grant you daily opportunities to discover anew the splendor of him!

NOTES

1 Samuel Scudder (a Student), "Agassiz and the Fish," *American Poems, 3rd* ed. (Houghton, Osgood & Co., 1879), 450–54, quoted in Justin Taylor, "Agassiz and the Fish" (blog), *The Gospel Coalition*, November 16, 2009, https://www.thegospelcoalition.org/blogs/justin-taylor/agassiz-and-the-fish/.

2 A. W. Tozer, *The Knowledge of the Holy* (Harper & Row Publishers, 1961), 11.

3 J. D. Douglas et al, eds., *The Illustrated Bible Dictionary, vol. 1, Aaron-Golan* (Inter-Varsity Press, 1980), 151.

4 Jeff Miller, "The Aesthetic Argument for the Existence of God," *Apologetics Press*, September 2, 2017, https://apologeticspress.org/the-aesthetic-argument-for-the-existence-of-god-5451/.

5 Tozer, *The Knowledge of the Holy,* 39.

6 Ray Ortlund, "What Does the Bible Say about God as Our Father?" *Crossway*, June 19, 2022, https://www.crossway.org/articles/what-does-the-bible-say-about-god-as-our-father/.

7 *Strong's Concordance*, "1391. doxa," *Bible Hub,* https://biblehub.com/greek/1391.htm.

8 Tozer, *The Knowledge of the Holy,* 82, 84.

9 Lawrence O. Richards, *Expository Dictionary of Bible Words* (Regency Reference Library, 1985), 339.

10 Millard J. Erickson, *Christian Theology, 2nd ed.* (Baker Academic, 1983, 1998), 329.

11 Tozer, *The Knowledge of the Holy,* 46.

12 Wayne Grudem, "Guide to the Attributes of God," *Zondervan Academic*, May 17, 2018, https://zondervanacademic.com/blog/attributes-of-god.

13 Wayne Grudem, *Systematic Theology: An Introduction to Biblical Doctrine* (Inter-Varsity Press, 1994), 175–76.

14 Grudem, *Systematic Theology,* 192.

15 J. D. Douglas et al, eds., *The Illustrated Bible Dictionary, vol. 3, Parable-Zuzim,* 1159.

16 Richards, *Expository Dictionary,* 479.

17 Michael Horton, *The Christian Faith: A Systematic Theology for Pilgrims on the Way* (Zondervan, 2011), 228.

18 Horton, *The Christian Faith,* 230.

19 Erickson, *Christian Theology*, 316.

MADE EASY

by Rose Publishing

BIBLE STUDY MADE EASY

HOW WE GOT THE BIBLE MADE EASY

UNDERSTANDING THE HOLY SPIRIT MADE EASY

BIBLE CHRONOLOGY MADE EASY

THE BOOKS OF THE BIBLE MADE EASY

KNOWING GOD'S WILL MADE EASY

WORLD RELIGIONS MADE EASY

BASICS OF THE CHRISTIAN FAITH MADE EASY

SHARING YOUR FAITH MADE EASY

BIBLE TRANSLATIONS MADE EASY

BOOK OF REVELATION MADE EASY

WHO'S WHO IN THE BIBLE MADE EASY

SCRIPTURE MEMORY MADE EASY

END TIMES MADE EASY

CHRISTIAN DENOMINATIONS MADE EASY

ATTRIBUTES OF GOD MADE EASY

rose-publishing.com